Where's Your Tooth?

"Where's your tooth?" asked Dad.
"Is it under the pillow?"

"Where's your tooth?" asked Mom.
"Is it under the bed?"

"Where's your tooth?" asked Grandma.
"Is it under the chair?"

"Where's your tooth?" asked Grandpa.
"Is it under the bear?"

"Where's your tooth?"

"Where's your tooth?"

"Here's your tooth!" said the tooth fairy.